T0045496

The Speedy Cheetah

Rachel Elliott

A cheetah is a kind of wild cat.
Cheetahs live in Africa.

AFRICA

A cheetah looks like a very large cat.
A cheetah weighs about 120 pounds.

7-year-old boy

cheetah

120 pounds

55 pounds

A cheetah has a long body.
Its body is about 4 feet long.

house cat

$1\frac{1}{2}$ feet

0   1   2   3   4

4 feet

cheetah

A cheetah stands on 4 legs.
It grows to be about 3 feet tall.

7-year-old boy

4 feet

4

cheetah

3 feet

3

2

1

0

A cheetah has strong legs.
It can run as fast as a car on a highway.

cheetah

60 miles an hour

car

Baby cheetahs are called cubs.

The cubs soon grow up.

They become fast and beautiful cheetahs.